Legal & Disclaimer

The information contained in this book and its contents is not desig f any form of medical or professional advice; and is not meant to replace the need for independent medical, financial, legal or other professional advice or services, as may be required. The content and information in this book has been provided for educational and entertainment purposes only.

The content and information contained in this book has been compiled from sources deemed reliable, and it is accurate to the best of the Author's knowledge, information and belief. However, the Author cannot guarantee its accuracy and validity and cannot be held liable for any errors and/or omissions. Further, changes are periodically made to this book as and when needed. Where appropriate and/or necessary, you must consult a professional (including but not limited to your doctor, attorney, financial advisor or such other professional advisor) before using any of the suggested remedies, techniques, or information in this book.

CONTENTS

INTRODUCTION

A diverticulitis diet is something your doctor might recommend as part of a short-term treatment plan for acute diverticulitis.

Diverticula are small, bulging pouches that can form in the lining of the digestive system. They're found most often in the lower part of the large intestine (colon). This condition is called diverticulosis.

In some cases, one or more of the pouches become inflamed or infected. This is known as diverticulitis.

Mild cases of diverticulitis are usually treated with antibiotics and a low-fiber diet, or treatment may start with a period of rest where you eat nothing by mouth, then start with clear liquids and then move to a low-fiber diet until your condition improves. More-severe cases typically require hospitalization.

Nutrition therapy for diverticulitis is a temporary measure to give your digestive system a chance to rest. Eat small amounts until bleeding and diarrhea subside.

Diet details

Your diet starts with only clear liquids for a few days. Examples of items allowed on a clear liquid diet include:

- Broth
- Fruit juices without pulp, such as apple juice
- Ice chips
- Ice pops without bits of fruit or fruit pulp
- Gelatin
- Water
- Tea or coffee without cream

As you start feeling better, your doctor will recommend that you slowly add low-fiber foods. Examples of low-fiber foods include:

- Canned or cooked fruits without skin or seeds
- Canned or cooked vegetables such as green beans, carrots and potatoes (without the skin)
- Eggs, fish and poultry
- Refined white bread

- Fruit and vegetable juice with no pulp
- Low-fiber cereals
- Milk, yogurt and cheese
- White rice, pasta and noodles

Results

You should feel better within two or three days of starting the diet and antibiotics. If you haven't started feeling better by then, call your doctor. Also contact your doctor if:

- You develop a fever
- Your abdominal pain is worsening
- You're unable to keep clear liquids down

These may indicate a complication that requires hospitalization.

Risks

Nutrition therapy for diverticulitis has few risks. However, continuing a clear liquid diet for more than a few days can lead to weakness and other complications, since it doesn't provide enough of the nutrients your body needs. For this reason, your doctor will want you to transition back to a normal diet that includes foods with fiber as soon as you can tolerate it.

14-Day Meal Plan

Meal Plan	Breakfast	Lunch	Dinner
Day-1	Apple Raisin Pancakes	Apple Chicken Pita Pocket	Chicken Florentine
Day-2	Asparagus and Bean Frittata	Bean and Mushroom Stew	Pasta with Beans and Turkey
Day-3	Banana Bran Muffins	Bean Enchiladas	Grilled Steak with Spinach and Apple Salad
Day-4	Banana Breakfast Smoothie	Beef Fajitas	Quick Broccoli Pasta Toss
Day-5	Breakfast Carrot Cake	Broccoli and Mushroom Brown Rice	Summer Spaghetti
Day-6	Carrot and Zucchini Bread	Chicken and Asparagus Pasta	Vegetable and Butternut Squash Curry
Day-7	Oatmeal Pumpkin Raisin Pancakes	Vegetable and Garbanzo Curry	Vegeterian Penne Pasta
Day-8	Sante Fe Omelet	Couscous with Vegetables	Creamy Carrot Soup
Day-9	Tropical Fruit Smoothie	Chicken Pasta Salad	Mediterranean Salmon and Potato Salad
Day-10	Zucchini and Bean Scramble	Pasta with Chicken and Olives	Southwestern Chicken Pitas
Day-11	Greek Lettuce Wraps	Chipotle Black Bean Chili	Spinach and Ham Pizza
Day-12	Bean and Tomato Salad	Asian Chicken Salad	Vegetable and Butternut Squash Curry
Day-13	Delicious Sweet Potatoes	Ziti with Zesty Chicken	Baked Artichoke Dip
Day-14	Tortellini with Navy Bean Sauce	Quick Spinach and Black Bean Salad	Spinach and Mushroom Toss

BREAKFAST RECIPES

Apple Raisin Pancakes

An alternative to traditional pancakes with a lot more fiber per serving.
Serves: 4 pancakes

Ingredients:

- 2 eggs
- 1 Cup unsweetened applesauce
- 1 Teaspoon cinnamon
- 2 Teaspoons brown sugar
- 1 Cup wheat flour
- 1/2 Cup white flour
- 2 Teaspoons baking powder
- 2 Teaspoons vanilla
- 1/2 Cup golden, seedless raisins
- non-stick cooking spray

Directions:

In a medium bowl, beat eggs until fluffy. Add applesauce, cinnamon, sugar, flours, baking powder, vanilla and raisins and continue to stir just until smooth. Heat griddle or pan over medium heat. Spray with non-stick cooking spray. For each pancake, pour about 1/4 cup of batter into hot pan. Cook pancakes until edges get puffy. Turn and cook other side unti golden. Serve pancakes with additional applesauce if desired.

Asparagus and Bean Frittata

Filled with lots of flavor and fiber, you'll enjoy this at breakfast or anytime.
Serves: 4

Ingredients:

- 2 Tablespoons olive oil
- 1 Cup onion, chopped
- 1 Cup red pepper, seeded, chopped
- 1 garlic clove, minced
- 14 Ounces can red or black or white beans, drained, rinsed
- 1 Cup asparagus, cooked and chopped
- 4 eggs
- 1/2 Teaspoon salt
- 1/4 Cup Parmesan cheese

Directions:

Preheat oven to 350 degrees.

In a large oven-proof pan, heat 1 tbsp olive oil over medium-high heat. Cook onions, red peppers, garlic, and red beans until vegetables are soft (about 10 minutes). Set aside.

In medium bowl, beat eggs and salt, then add asparagus; set aside.

Add remaining 1 tbsp olive oil into the vegetable pan and pour in the egg mixture. Reduce heat to medium-low and cook for 10 to 15 minutes, or until mixture is set on bottom and lightly browned. Sprinkle Parmesan cheese over top of mixture and broil in the oven for an additional 3 to 5 minutes or until cheese is lightly browned and eggs are cooked through.

Banana Bran Muffins

These muffins provide a good amount of fiber, necessary in the diverticulosis diet.
Serves: 12 muffins

Ingredients:

- 1 1/2 Cup All-Bran cereal
- 2/3 Cups milk
- 4 eggs
- 1/4 Cup canola oil
- 1 Cup ripe banana, mashed (about 2 bananas)
- 1/2 Cup brown sugar
- 1 Cup whole wheat flour
- 2 Teaspoons baking powder
- 1/2 Teaspoon salt

Directions:

Preheat oven to 400F degrees.
In a large bowl, combine All-Bran cereal and milk and set aside. Add eggs and oil; stir in mashed banana and brown sugar and combine well. In a separate small bowl, combine flour, baking powder and salt. Add dry ingredients to banana mixture, stirring just until combined. Pour batter evenly into 12 greased or paper-lined muffin tins; Bake 15 to 18 minutes or until golden-brown and firm. Allow to cool prior to serving.

Banana Breakfast Smoothie

This smoothie tastes great and easy to make.
Serves:1 Smoothie

Ingredients:

- 1 medium banana
- 1 Cup milk, almond or regular
- 1/2 Cup plain yogurt
- 1/4 Cup 100% Bran flakes
- 1 Teaspoon vanilla extract
- 2 Teaspoons honey or agave syrup
- 1/2 Cup ice
- 1 Pinch cinnamon
- 1 Pinch nutmeg

Directions:

Combine all ingredients in a blender and process on medium speed until smooth. Garnish with cinnamon and/or nutmeg.

Breakfast Carrot Cake

This carrot cake is high in fiber and delicious. Make some over the weekend, and enjoy on weekday busy mornings.

Serves: 8-10 slices

Ingredients:

- 1 1/3 Cup water
- 1/2 Cup brown sugar
- 1 Cup seedless raisins
- 2 carrots, grated
- 1 apple, unpeeled, chopped
- 1 Teaspoon cinnamon
- 1 Teaspoon ground cloves
- 1 Teaspoon nutmeg
- 2 Teaspoons butter
- 2 Cups whole wheat flour
- 1 Teaspoon baking soda

Directions:

Preheat oven to 375F degrees. Spray a 9x5 inch loaf pan with non-stick cooking spray.

In a medium saucepan, over low heat, mix together water, sugar, raisins, carrots, apples, cinnamon, cloves, nutmeg, and butter. Cook for 5-7 minutes, until well combined, and sugar dissolves. Remove pan from heat and allow to cool.

In a large bowl, combine flour, baking soda and salt. Stir carrot mixture into flour mixture and mix just until combined. Pour into prepared pan. Bake for 1 1/4 hours, or until a knife inserted in the center comes out clean. Cool on wire rack.

Carrot and Zucchini Bread

Packed with lots of fiber and goodness, make these two loaves on the weekend and enjoy during the week, or consider giving one loaf to a friend.

Serves: 2 loaves

Ingredients:

- 3 1/2 Cups whole wheat flour
- 1 Tablespoon baking powder
- 1 Teaspoon baking soda
- 1/2 Teaspoon salt
- 1 Teaspoon cinnamon
- 2 eggs, lightly beaten
- 1 1/2 Cup buttermilk
- 2 Tablespoons butter, melted
- 1/2 Cup brown sugar
- 1 Cup zucchini, unpeeled, grated
- 1 Cup carrot, grated
- 1 Cup apple, unseeded, grated

Directions:

Preheat oven to 350F degrees.

Spray two 9x5-inch loaf pans with non-stick cooking spray. In a bowl, combine the flour, baking powder, baking soda, salt, and cinnamon; set aside.

In a large, separate bowl, combine the eggs, buttermilk, and melted butter. Stir in the brown sugar. Add the zucchini, carrots, and apple and combine.

Stir in the dry ingredients into the wet ingredients and stir gently until just combined.

Pour batter into prepared loaf pans. Bake for 60 minutes, or until a knife inserted into the center of the loaf comes out clean. Cool loaves in the pan for 10 minutes before removing to a wire rack to cool completely

Oatmeal Pumpkin Raisin Pancakes

Easy to make pancakes with loads of fiber and a little sweetness with the fruit.
Serves: 6-8 pancakes

Ingredients:

- 1 1/2 Cup rolled oats
- 1/2 Cup whole wheat flour
- 1 Tablespoon baking powder
- 1 Teaspoon cinnamon
- 1 Teaspoon nutmeg
- 1 egg
- 1 banana, mashed
- 1 Tablespoon honey
- 1/2 Cup pumpkin puree, canned
- 1 1/2 Cup milk
- 1/2 Cup seedless raisins
- Non-stick cooking spray

Directions:

In a large bowl mix together oats, whole wheat flour, baking powder, cinnamon, and nutmeg. Set aside. In a separate bowl, mix together egg, banana, honey, pumpkin puree, milk and raisins or dates. Mix dry mixture into wet mixture. Heat griddle or skillet over medium heat. Spray with non-stick cooking spray. For each pancake, pour slightly less than 1/4 cup batter from cup into hot griddle or pan. Cook pancakes until puffed and dry around edges. Turn and cook other side until golden.

Sante Fe Omelet

This omelet is a great savory breakfast with plenty of fiber.
Serves: 2

Ingredients:

- 4 eggs
- 2 Tablespoons milk or water
- 1/4 Teaspoon salt
- 1 1/2 Tablespoon butter
- 1/2 Cup red beans, drained, rinsed
- 1 tomato, seeded, chopped
- 1/2 Cup green bell pepper, seeded, chopped
- 2 Tablespoons cheddar cheese, grated
- 2 Pieces whole wheat tortillas

Directions:

In a medium bowl, whisk together eggs, milk or water and salt. Heat butter in a medium skillet and add red beans. Cook for 3 minutes, add tomatoes and green peppers. Cook for another 5 minutes until vegetables soften. Pour in egg mixture and sprinkle the cheese over the eggs. Cover until cheese melts. Serve with whole wheat tortillas.

Tropical Fruit Smoothie

This easy to make smoothie can be made with any seasonal fruit...peaches, pineapples, mangoes, bananas.

Serves: 2

Ingredients:

- 1 Cup mix of mangoes, pineapples, bananas
- 1 Cup plain or vanilla yogurt
- 1/2 Cup All Bran cereal
- 1 Teaspoon vanilla
- 1 Tablespoon honey, or agave nectar, optional
- 1 Cup almond or coconut milk or water
- 1/2 avocado
- 1 Cup ice

Directions:

Combine all ingredients in a blender and process on high speed until smooth and creamy.

Zucchini and Bean Scramble

A vegetarian alternative to a traditional omelet with lots of fiber and flavor.

Serves: 4

Ingredients:

- 2 Tablespoons olive oil
- 1/2 Cup red onions, chopped finely
- 1 medium zucchini, seeded, chopped
- 14 Ounces can black beans, drained, rinsed
- 1/2 tomato, seeded, chopped
- 4 eggs
- 1/4 Cup milk
- 1 Teaspoon salt
- 4 whole wheat English muffins

Directions:

In a large non-stick pan, heat olive oil over moderate heat.

Add onions, zucchini, black beans and tomato. Cook for 5-10 minutes or until vegetables are soft. In a separate bowl, mix together eggs and milk and salt. Add egg mixture to pan and stir to cook through, about 5 minutes. Serve with whole wheat English muffins.

MAIN COURSE RECIPES

Apple Chicken Pita Pocket

You can make this salad the night before and just fill the pitas in the morning.
Serves: 4

Ingredients:

- 2 Cups chicken, cooked, cubed
- 2 apples, unpeeled, chopped
- 1 celery stalk, chopped
- 1/3 Cup plain yogurt
- 1/4 Cup mayonaise
- 4 round whole wheat pita breads
- 4 romaine lettuce leaves

Directions:

In a medium bowl, combine the chicken, apples, and celery.
Add yogurt and mayonnaise. Mix well. Slice pita to make a pocket. Line with lettuce leaf and fill pita pocket with 1 cup of mixture per pita bread. Serve with mixed fruit salad (no berries).

Bean and Mushroom Stew

Although this dish can be eaten on its own, it would be delicious over brown rice.

Serves: 4

Ingredients:

- 2 Tablespoons olive oil
- 1 Pound white mushrooms, sliced
- 1 Cup onion, chopped
- 1 Teaspoon garlic cloves, minced
- 3/4 Teaspoons dried thyme
- 28 Ounces chicken broth
- 14 Ounces can stewed tomatoes, chopped
- 1/4 Cup white wine, optional
- 30 Ounces can,cannellini beans, drained and rinsed

Directions:

In a large saucepan, heat olive oil over medium high heat. Cook mushrooms, onion, garlic and thyme until onion is tender and mushrooms are slightly golden (about 7 minutes). Add chicken broth, tomatoes and wine and bring to a boil. Cover and simmer for about 35 additional minutes. In a small bowl, mash 1 cup of the beans until smooth; add to stew. Stir in remaining beans, heat until hot. Serve immediately with a side of cooked long grain rice, if desired.

Bean Enchiladas

The beans and the whole wheat tortillas transform this dish into a high fiber, yummy dish.
Serves: 4

Ingredients:

- 14 Ounces can red beans, drained, rinsed, mashed
- 2 Cups cheddar cheese, grated
- 1/2 Cup onion, chopped
- 1/4 Cup black olives, sliced
- 2 Cups tomato sauce
- 2 Teaspoons garlic salt
- 8 whole wheat tortillas

Directions:

Preheat oven to 350F degrees.
In a medium bowl, combine the mashed beans, cheese, onions, olives, one cup tomato sauce, and garlic salt. Place about 1/3 cup bean mixture along center of each tortilla. Roll up and place enchiladas in large baking dish. Spoon remaining tomato sauce on top of the filled tortillas. Sprinkle with additional cheese, if desired. Bake for 15 to 20 minutes or until thoroughly heated.

Beef Fajitas

The use of vegetables and whole wheat flour tortillas make this a healthier version of fajitas.
Serves: 4 Fajitas

Ingredients:

- 6 Ounces flank steak, trimmed of fat
- 2 Teaspoons lime juice
- 1 Teaspoon garlic, chopped
- 1 Teaspoon olive oil, divided
- 15 Ounces can red beans, drained, rinsed, mashed
- 1/2 Cup medium green pepper, seeded and thinly sliced
- 1/2 Cup red bell pepper, thinly sliced
- 1 Tablespoon scallions, chopped
- 4 whole wheat tortillas

Directions:

Season flank steak with salt. Let sit for 10 minutes. Grill flank steak over high heat until cooked on both sides. Place steak on separate plate to rest for 10 minutes. Cut flank steak into thin strips against the grain. In a small bowl, whisk together lime juice, garlic, and 1/2 teaspoon of olive oil. Set aside.
In a small pan, heat the other 1/2 tsp olive oil and combine beans, bell peppers and scallions and heat through. To assemble fajitas, take tortilla and place steak inside. Top with bean mixture and drizzle some of the lime sauce on top. Roll into fajita and serve immediately.

Broccoli and Mushroom Brown Rice

Although this is a vegetarian meal, the portobello mushrooms give this dish a meaty texture.
Serves: 4

Ingredients:

- 1 Tablespoon olive oil
- 1 medium onion, chopped
- 2 garlic cloves, minced
- 1 Cup instant brown rice
- 8 Ounces Portobello mushrooms, sliced
- 3/4 Cups vegetable broth
- 1 Pound broccoli florets, fresh, cut into bite-size pieces
- 1/2 Teaspoon salt
- 1/4 Teaspoon pepper

Directions:

In a medium pan, heat olive oil over medium-high heat. Cook onions and garlic until translucent, about 5 minutes. Stir in rice and mushrooms and cook 3-5 minutes or until mushrooms have released all of their juices. Add the broth and bring to a boil. Reduce heat to medium-low and cover until liquid is absorbed (about 7 - 8 minutes). Place broccoli florets in a microwave-safe casserole dish and sprinkle with salt and pepper and add 4 tbs. water. Cover and cook at high power for 5 to 7 minutes or until tender. Fluff rice with a fork and pour into a serving platter and top with broccoli. Toss to combine and serve. Can be topped with freshly grated Parmesan cheese and fresh Italian parsley.

Chicken and Asparagus Pasta

Serves: 4

Ingredients:

- 1 Pound whole wheat penne pasta
- 2 Tablespoons olive oil
- 1 Pound chicken breast halves, boneless and sliced into strips
- 1/2 Teaspoon poultry seasoning
- 4 Pieces garlic cloves, minced
- 1 1/2 Cup asparagus, frozen, thawed, cut into 1 inch pieces
- 1 Cup peas, frozen, thawed
- 1/4 Cup Parmesan cheese, grated

Directions:

Bring a large pot of salted water to boil. Add pasta and cook al dente according to package directions. Heat one tablespoon olive oil in a pan over medium heat and cook chicken with poultry seasoning until golden. Remove cooked chicken from the pan. Add the remaining tablespoon of olive oil, garlic, asparagus and peas. Cook until vegetables are tender. Place chicken back in with the asparagus mixture and cook together for 2 minutes or until heated through. Place pasta in a large shallow pasta bowl and toss with chicken mixture. Top with parmesan cheese.

Chicken Florentine

Serves: 4

Ingredients:

- 2 Tablespoons olive oil
- 2 zucchinis, seeded, thinly sliced
- 1/2 Cup green onion, sliced
- 2 chicken breast, cubed
- 1/2 Teaspoon salt
- 1/2 Teaspoon thyme, ground
- 3 Cups long grain rice, cooked
- 4 Cups fresh spinach, chopped
- 1/4 Cup Parmesan cheese, grated

Directions:

In a medium pan, heat olive oil over medium heat. Add zucchini, onions, and chicken, stirring occasionally for 5 to 10 minutes, or until chicken is golden. Add salt, thyme, rice and spinach. Cook and stir for another 6 - 8 minutes or until heated through and spinach wilts. Remove from heat, transfer to a large serving bowl, and stir in cheese. Serve.

Chipotle Black Bean Chili

This chili is delicious and loaded with fiber and Southwest flavor.

Serves: 4

Ingredients:

- 1 Tablespoon olive oil
- 1 Cup onion, finely chopped
- garlic cloves, minced
- 1/2 Teaspoon chipotle powder
- 1/2 Teaspoon cumin
- 1/4 Teaspoon salt
- 30 Ounces can black beans, drained and rinsed
- 28 Ounces tomatoes, seeded, chopped
- 1 Teaspoon fresh cilantro

Directions:

In a large non-stick pan, heat olive oil over medium heat. Add onions and garlic and cook 5 minutes or until they are soft. Add chipotle powder, cumin, salt, beans, and tomatoes bring to a boil. Reduce heat, cover and simmer 15-25 or until chili thickens. Garnish with fresh cilantro.

Cottage Crunch Wraps

This is a quick and easy recipe either for a lunch or a snack.
Serves: 2

Ingredients:

- 3/4 Cups cottage cheese
- 1/4 Cup carrots, shredded
- green onion, sliced
- 1/2 Cup tomatoes, seeded, chopped
- 1/2 Cup cabbage, chopped
- 1 Teaspoon lime juice
- whole wheat tortillas

Directions:

In a medium bowl, place cheese, carrots, onions, tomatoes, and cabbage and mix well. Add lime juice. Place mixture in tortillas, wrap and serve.

Couscous with Vegetables

This vegetarian meal is a great alternative to rice or pasta and still has lots of fiber.
Serves: 4

Ingredients:

- 1 1/2 Cup chicken broth
- 1 Cup couscous
- 4 Tablespoons olive oil, divided
- red onion, chopped
- garlic cloves, minced
- tomatoes, seeded, chopped
- yellow bell pepper, seeded and chopped
- red bell pepper, seeded and chopped
- zucchinis, seeded, chopped
- 1 Cup peas, thawed from frozen
- 2 Tablespoons balsamic vinegar
- 2 Tablespoons Feta cheese, crumbled

Directions:

In a medium saucepan, over high heat, bring chicken broth and 1 tbs of olive oil to a boil. Remove from heat and stir in couscous. Cover and let sit for 5-10 minutes.

In a separate pan over medium heat, add the remaining oil and cook the onions and garlic until softened. Mix in the tomatoes, bell peppers and zucchinis. Cook and stir until tender. Add peas and cook 2-3 more minutes. Add vinegar and cheese and toss to combine. Spoon vegetable mixture over couscous. Serve.

Garbanzo Pita Pockets

This will become a go to recipe for a quick and healthy, high fiber snack or lunch that requires no cooking.

Serves: 4

Ingredients:

- 15 Ounces can garbanzo beans, drained, rinsed
- 6 Ounces can artichokes, marinated, quartered, liquid reserved
- 1 Tablespoon black olives. sliced
- 1 Tablespoon green olives, sliced
- green bell pepper, seeded, chopped
- red bell pepper, seeded and chopped
- small red onion, thinly sliced
- 2 Tablespoons red wine vinegar
- 1/2 Cup fresh basil, chopped
- whole wheat pita pockets

Directions:

In a large bowl, combine the garbanzo beans, artichokes and their liquid, olives, garlic, peppers, onion, vinegar and basil. Mix well and set aside. Slice pita bread to make a pocket. Place a lettuce leaf in each pita and fill with the garbanzo filling. Serve.

Grilled Steak with Spinach and Apple Salad

An easy way to get meat, vegetables and fiber in a meal.
Serves: 2

Ingredients:

- beef steaks, rib-eye or sirloin
- 4 Tablespoons olive oil
- salt and pepper to taste
- 1 Tablespoon balsamic vinegar
- 2 Cups fresh baby spinach, washed and dried
- apple (preferably tart, like Granny Smith), unpeeled and sliced
- 4 Ounces Parmesan cheese, grated

Directions:

Prepare steaks for grill by pouring 2 tbs olive oil and salt to taste. Grill over high heat to desired doneness, about 7 minutes per side for medium. Once cooked, place steaks on plate to rest and let juices redistribute without cutting.

To make dressing, in a small bowl, whisk together balsamic vinegar, 2 tbs olive oil and salt and pepper to taste.

On individual plates, stack spinach, apples and steak that have been cut diagonally. Drizzle with dressing and top with Parmesan cheese.

Lentil Risotto

This risotto is delicious and has fiber due to the added lentils.

Ingredients:

- 2 Tablespoons olive oil
- medium leeks, chopped
- garlic cloves, minced
- red bell pepper, seeded and chopped
- 3 Cups chicken broth
- 1 1/4 Cup long grain rice
- 1 Tablespoon fresh basil, chopped
- 1 Cup lentils, cooked
- 1/4 Cup Italian parsley, chopped
- 1/4 Cup Parmesan cheese, grated

Directions:

In a large pot, heat olive oil over moderate heat and cook leeks, garlic, and red pepper until softened. Add broth along with the rice, and basil. Cover and let simmer until rice is done then add cooked lentils and stir for 10 minutes. Remove from heat and add parsley and parmesan cheese. Serve.

Pasta with Beans and Turkey

Serves: 4

Ingredients:

- 1 Pound whole wheat pasta
- 1 Tablespoon olive oil
- onion
- garlic cloves, minced
- 1 Pound ground turkey
- small head escarole, rinsed, drained, and chopped
- 14 Ounces can,cannellini beans, drained and rinsed
- 1 1/2 Cup chicken broth
- 1 Tablespoon fresh rosemary, chopped
- 1/2 Teaspoon salt
- 1/2 Teaspoon pepper
- 1/2 Cup Parmesan cheese

Directions:

Bring a large pot of salted water to boil. Add pasta and cook according to package directions. Drain. In a large pan, heat olive oil over medium heat. Add onion and cook until softened, add garlic and turkey and cook until it browns, about 5-7 minutes. Add the escarole and cook until wilted, about 3 to 4 minutes. Add the beans, 1 cup of chicken stock, rosemary, and salt and pepper. Simmer until the mixture is slightly thickened. Add the turkey-bean mixture to pasta and toss well, thinning sauce with the additional 1/2 cup chicken stock if necessary. Top with parmesan cheese. Serve.

Pasta with Chicken and Olives

This meal is easy to pull together and has an unique flavor with the olives and rosemary.
Serves: 4

Ingredients:

- 1 Pound whole wheat pasta
- 2 Tablespoons olive oil
- onion, chopped
- garlic cloves, minced
- 1 Pound chicken breast, cut into chunks
- 1 Teaspoon dried basil
- 1 Teaspoon dried rosemary
- black olives, sliced
- green bell pepper, seeded, chopped
- 14 Ounces can stewed tomatoes, chopped
- 2 Cups chicken broth
- 1/2 Cup Romano cheese

Directions:

Bring a large pot of salted water to boil. Add pasta and cook according to package directions until al dente. While pasta
is cooking, heat the oil in a large pan over medium heat. Add the onion and garlic and cook until the onion is tender, about 6 minutes. Add the chicken, basil and rosemary and cook until the chicken is lightly browned, about 8 minutes. Stir in the olives, green pepper and tomatoes and cook until the tomatoes begin to give off liquid, about 2 minutes.

Add the chicken broth to the pan, heat pan to boiling and boil until half of the liquid is evaporated, about 5-7 minutes. When pasta is done, add to sauce mixture. Toss until pasta is evenly mixed with sauce. Top with cheese and serve.

Quick Broccoli Pasta Toss

This is a super easy one pot meal loaded with lots of fiber and just a few ingredients.
Serves: 2

Ingredients:

- 2 Cups broccoli florets, fresh or thawed if frozen
- 1/2 p Pound whole wheat pasta
- 1/2 Tablespoon olive oil
- 1 1/2 Tablespoon Parmesan cheese
- 1/8 Teaspoon garlic powder

Directions:

Bring a large pot of salted water to a boil. Add broccoli and pasta and cook for about 6 - 8 minutes or until tender. Drain well. Place pasta mixture in a large shallow pasta bowl and toss with olive oil, cheese and garlic powder. Serve.

Rice and Vegetable Casserole

This recipe can be vegetarian or beef, chicken or seafood can be added for some added protein.
Serves: 4

Ingredients:

- Non-stick cooking spray
- 1 Cup long-grain brown rice
- 1/4 Cup mushrooms, sliced
- 1/4 Cup broccoli, chopped
- 1/4 Cup carrots, chopped
- 1/4 Cup red bell pepper, seeded and chopped
- 1/4 Cup onion, finely chopped
- 1 Teaspoon salt
- 1 Teaspoon paprika
- 1 Teaspoon oregano
- 2-2 1/2 Cups vegetable broth
- 1/4 Cup cheddar cheese, shredded

Directions:

Preheat oven to 425 degrees.
Spray a 13x9 glass baking dish lightly with non-stick cooking spray.
In a large bowl, combine brown rice, mushrooms, broccoli, carrots, bell pepper, onion, salt, paprika, oregano and broth. Mix well and cover with foil. Bake in preheated oven for 30 minutes, or until cooked through; stir once half way during baking. Top with shredded cheddar cheese and allow it to melt prior to serving.

Roasted Chicken and Vegetables

An easy recipe with lots of flavor and fiber but not a lot of fuss.
Serves: 4

Ingredients:

- Roma tomatoes, seedless, quartered
- zucchini, medium, chopped coarsely
- potatoes, large, unpeeled, quartered
- 3 Tablespoons olive oil, divided
- 3/4 Teaspoons salt, divided
- garlic cloves, minced
- 1 Tablespoon fresh rosemary, chopped
- 1 Tablespoon fresh thyme, taken off sprig
- 1 Teaspoon lemon zest
- 1 Tablespoon lemon juice
- chicken breast halves, skinless

Directions:

Preheat oven to 375F degrees.

Place tomatoes, zucchini and potatoes in a large roasting pan, and toss with 2 tbs of oil and 1/4 tsp salt. In a small bowl, combine 1 tbs oil, 1/2 tsp salt, garlic, rosemary, thyme, lemon zest and lemon juice. Pour this mixture over chicken. Place chicken in pan with vegetables. Bake in oven for 30 minutes. Stir chicken and vegetables and bake another 25 minutes, or until chicken is cooked through and vegetables are tender.

Southwestern Chicken Pitas

An easy recipe that can be served at lunch or dinner, packed with flavor and fiber.
Serves: 6

Ingredients:

- 15 Ounces black beans, drained and rinsed
- 1/2 Cup red bell pepper, seeded and chopped
- 3 Tablespoons fresh lemon juice
- 2 Tablespoons fersh cilantro, minced
- 2 Teaspoons olive oil
- chicken breast halves, skinless
- round whole wheat pita pockets
- Monterrey Jack cheese, slices

Directions:

In a bowl, combine beans, bell pepper, lime juice, and cilantro. Set aside. In a large pan, heat canola oil over medium-high heat. Cook chicken in pan until golden brown. Set aside for 10 without cutting. Warm pita bread in oven. Cut chicken into slices. For each sandwich, place cheese slice halves down center of one pita bread. Top with chicken breast slices and bean mixture. Roll up tightly. Cut in half and serve.

Spinach and Ham Pizza

Here is a healthy alternative to regular pizza with much more flavor, fiber and nutrition.

Serves: 4

Prep time: 15m

Cook Time: 12m

Ingredients:

- 1 store bought baked thin crust whole wheat pizza shell
- 4 Cups baby spinach leaves, sliced thinly
- 1/2 Cup Mushrooms
- 2 Tablespoons olive oil
- 3 Ounces ham or prosciutto
- 1/4 Cup feta cheese, crumbled
- 1/4 Cup Parmesan cheese, grated
- 3 Pieces garlic cloves, sliced thinly

Directions:

Preheat oven to 450F degrees.

Place the pizza shell on a cookie sheet. Scatter spinach and mushrooms all over crust. Drizzle with oil. Place ham or prosciutto, cheeses, and garlic on top of spinach & mushroom. Bake for 10-12 minutes, until crust is golden brown and spinach is wilted.

Summer Spaghetti

The best time to make this is when the summer vegetables are in season, however, it can be enjoyed anytime of the year.

Serves: 4

Ingredients:

- 1 Pound whole wheat spaghetti
- 1/4 Cup olive oil
- shallot, minced
- garlic cloves, minced
- medium zucchini, chopped
- medium summer squash, chopped
- 1/4 Cup fresh basil, chopped
- 1/2 Teaspoon salt
- medium lemon, juiced
- 2 Tablespoons butter, room temperature
- freshly grated lemon peel

Directions:

Bring a large pot of salted water to boil. Add pasta and cook according to package directions until al dente.

In a large pan, heat oil over medium heat and cook the shallot and garlic stirring frequently.

Add the zucchini, squash, and basil. Continue to cook, stirring occasionally, until all vegetables are tender. Season with salt and lemon juice. Immediately place the sautéed vegetables with all their juices in a large shallow pasta bowl. Add the linguine and butter, toss to mix well and serve immediately. Top with freshly grated lemon peel.

Tortellini with Navy Bean Sauce

This sauce which is in a bean base, provides lots of fiber and a creamy texture to the tortellini.
Serves: 4

Ingredients:

- 2 Cups navy or white beans, dry, uncooked
- 2 Tablespoons olive oil
- small onion, chopped
- garlic cloves, minced
- 1 Cup tomatoes, seeded and chopped
- 2 Tablespoons tomato paste
- 7 Cups chicken broth
- bay leaf
- 1 Pound tortellini, store bought, filling of your choice
- 1/4 Cup fresh basil, chopped

Directions:

Cover the beans with water and soak for at least 8 hours or overnight. Drain.
In a non-stick pan, heat olive oil over medium heat. Add the onion and cook, for 3 minutes. Mix in the garlic and cook for another minute. Add the tomatoes and tomato paste, stir and cook for a few minutes. Add chicken broth, bay leaf and beans and bring to a boil, reduce the heat and simmer, uncovered, for 1 1/2 hours. Pour the bean mixture into a blender or food processor and process into a puree. Adjust the consistency with more stock if necessary. Bring large pot of salted water to boil. Cook tortellini according to package directions. Pour sauce over tortellini garnish with basil and serve.

Turkey and Barley Casserole

This recipe is versatile in that you can substitute chicken for the turkey and you can substitute any vegetables you have handy. It is an easy one pot meal and so delicious.
Serves: 4

Ingredients:

- 1 Pound ground turkey
- 1/2 Teaspoon salt
- small onion, chopped
- carrots, chopped
- celery stalks, chopped
- green bell pepper, seeded and chopped
- white button mushrooms, quartered
- 2 1/2 Cups chicken broth
- 1 Cup barley
- 1 Tablespoon poultry seasoning
- bay leaf

Directions:

Preheat oven to 375F degrees.
In a large pan, over medium- high heat, cook ground turkey with salt until browned, about 5 minutes. Add onions, carrots, celery and green peppers. Cook until tender, about 5 minutes. Add mushrooms, stock, barley, poultry seasoning and bay leaf. Mix together and place mixture in a 9x13 inch baking dish. Cover and bake in the preheated oven for 1 hour. Serve.

Vegetable and Butternut Squash Curry

Although an easy recipe, the exotic flavors of the curry powder and the richness of the coconut milk, will make this a favorite.
Serves: 4

Ingredients:

- 1 1/2 Pound butternut squash, seeded, peeled and chopped
- 1 Tablespoon olive oil
- onion, finely chopped
- 1 Tablespoon curry powder
- 1 2/3 Cup coconut milk
- 1 Cup water
- 3 Cups fresh spinach, chopped
- 14 Ounces butter beans, drained and rinsed
- 2 Tablespoons cilantro, chopped

Directions:

In a small saucepan, place squash and cover with water. Boil squash until tender and drain. In a large pan, heat olive oil and cook onions until tender. Stir in curry powder, continue stirring until fragrant, about 3 minutes. Stir in coconut milk and water.
Bring to boil; simmer, uncovered, about five minutes or until the mixture just thickens. Add squash, spinach, butter beans and cilantro. Stir until heated through. Serve.

Vegetable and Garbanzo Curry

The vegetables and brown rice in this dish pack a lot of fiber and the curry and ginger add a twist of flavor

Serves: 4

Ingredients:

- 2 Tablespoons vegetable oil
- 1 onion, sliced
- 2 Tablespoons curry powder
- 1/2 Teaspoon garlic powder
- 1/4 Teaspoon fresh ginger, grated
- 15 Ounces tomatoes, seeded and chopped
- 30 Ounces garbanzo beans, not drained
- 2 Cups potatoes, unpeeled, chopped
- 1 Cup carrots, sliced
- 2 Cups cauliflower, chopped
- 10 Ounces frozen peas, thawed
- 1/4 Teaspoon salt
- 1/4 Teaspoon pepper

Directions:

In a large non-stick pan, heat oil over medium-high heat. Cook onions until softened. Add curry powder, garlic powder and ginger; cook 2 minutes. Add tomatoes, garbanzo beans, potatoes, and carrots and stir together. Add cauliflower, cover and reduce heat to simmer. Cook for 20-30 minutes, until vegetable are tender, adding water if necessary. Stir in peas and salt and pepper; cook 5 more minutes. Serve over hot rice.

Vegeterian Penne Pasta

An easy way to get your fiber and vitamins in one dish. The whole wheat pasta has more fiber than traditional pasta.

Serves: 2

Ingredients:

- 1/2 Pound whole wheat penne or bowtie pasta
- 1 Tablespoon salt
- 2 Tablespoons olive oil
- 8 Ounces white mushrooms, sliced
- 8 Ounces asparagus, chopped
- 8 Ounces red bell pepper, seeded and chopped
- 1/4 Cup Parmesan cheese, grated
- 1/4 Cup fresh basil, chopped

Directions:

Bring a large pot of salted water to boil. Add pasta and cook according to package directions until al dente. Drain.

While the pasta is cooking, in a medium non-stick pan, heat olive oil over medium heat. Add the mushrooms and cook for about five minutes to release all the water. Add the asparagus and bell pepper and sauté for 3-4 minutes, until softened. Add cooked pasta to pan and add Parmesan cheese, stir until well combined. Transfer to a serving bowl, garnish with fresh basil and serve.

Ziti with Zesty Chicken

This dish is rich in flavor and the whole wheat pasta and peas add lots of fiber. Easy to make any day of the week.
Serves: 4

Ingredients:

- 1 Pound whole wheat ziti pasta or bowtie pasta
- 2 Teaspoons olive oil
- 1 onion, chopped
- 1 Tablespoon Dijon mustard
- 2 Tablespoons whole wheat flour
- 2 Cups chicken broth
- 1/4 Cup lemon juice
- 12 Ounces frozen peas, thawed
- 1/4 Cup fresh Italian parsley, chopped
- 12 Ounces cooked chicken, chopped

Directions:

Bring a large pot of salted water to a boil. Add pasta and cook according to package instructions until al dente. Drain. While pasta is cooking, in a large non-stick pan, heat olive oil over medium heat. Add the onion and cook for 3 minutes. Stir in the Dijon mustard and flour. Gradually whisk in the chicken broth, stirring constantly to avoid clumps. Bring the broth to a boil and stir in the lemon juice, peas and parsley. Add cooked pasta and cooked chicken to sauce and serve.

SOUP RECIPES

Asparagus Soup

This is an easy soup to make soup that has lots of flavor and fiber.
Serves: 4

Ingredients:

- 1 Tablespoon olive oil
- 1 Cup shallots, finely chopped
- 3 garlic cloves, minced
- 2 Pounds asparagus, chopped into one inch pieces
- 6 Cups vegetable stock
- 1 Teaspoon salt

Directions:

Reserve asparagus tops for later use. In a large soup pot, heat olive oil over medium heat. Cook shallots and garlic until softened, about 3-5 minutes. Add asparagus stalks, vegetable stock and salt and bring to a boil. Cover and reduce heat to low and simmer until asparagus softens. Let soup cool and puree with a hand blender, until creamy. Add asparagus tops and cook on medium for 5 minutes, until tops are tender.

Beans with Greens Soup

A hearty and fiber filled soup with easy to find ingredients.

Ingredients:

- 2 Tablespoons olive oil
- 1 onion, chopped
- 4 garlic cloves, minced
- 2 celery stalks, sliced finely
- 2 carrots, sliced
- 6 Cups chicken broth
- 1/4 Teaspoon thyme
- 1/4 Teaspoon rosemary
- 1 bay leaf
- 14 Ounces cannellini beans, drained and rinsed
- 1/2 Teaspoon salt
- 1 Cup leafy greens (kale, spinach or chard), chopped

Directions:

In a large soup pot, heat olive oil over medium heat. Add onions and cook until softened, about 3 minutes. Stir in onion, garlic, celery, and carrots and continue to cook for 5 minutes, stirring occasionally. Add chicken broth, thyme, rosemary, and bay leaf and cook until it comes to a boil. Reduce heat and cover and simmer gently for about 45-60 minutes.

Add beans and season with salt. Add leafy greens and cook until tender, approximately 5-10 minutes, depending on the greens being used. Serve.

For a creamier texture, prior to adding the greens, the broth and vegetables can be blended with an immersion blender until desired consistency is reached.

Beef and Vegetable Soup

This very easy one-pot soup can be made ahead of time and stored or it can be on the table in less than an hour. This has beef, but can be substituted with turkey or chicken and has lots of fiber, important in the diverticulosis diet.

Ingredients:

- 1/2 Pound stew beef, diced
- 1/2 bag frozen vegetable medley
- 1/4 Cup barley
- 32 Ounces beef broth
- 2 tomatoes, seeded and chopped
- 1 Teaspoon garlic powder
- 1 Teaspoon paprika
- 1 Teaspoon oregano
- 1 bay leaf
- 1 yellow or red potato, chopped

Directions:

In a large soup pot, over medium-high heat, brown ground beef. Add frozen vegetables, barley, broth, tomatoes, garlic powder, paprika, oregano and bay leaf. Bring the pot to a boil, Reduce heat, cover and simmer for 15 minutes. Add the potatoes and allow to simmer again for another 20 minutes or until they are tender

Cannellini and Butter Bean Soup

This bean based soup packs a lot of fiber, advised for diverticulosis, and the pancetta adds another layer of flavor.

Ingredients:

- 1 Tablespoon olive oil
- 3 slices pancetta, chopped
- 3 garlic cloves, minced
- 2 medium onions, chopped
- 28 Ounces cannellini beans, drained and rinsed
- 28 Ounces butter (lima) beans, drained and rinsed
- 2 Teaspoons thyme, fresh, chopped
- 1 Tablespoon balsamic vinegar
- 6 Cups vegetable stock

Directions:

In a large soup pot, heat olive oil over medium-high heat. Cook pancetta until crisp. Add garlic and onions. Cook until onions are tender, about 5 minutes. Stir in beans, thyme, vinegar and vegetable stock. Bring pot to a boil, reduce heat and simmer uncovered for 25 minutes. Serve.

Chicken and Split Pea Soup

This is one of the easiest, but flavorful one pot soup dishes. Perfect for dinner or to take for lunch.
Serves: 4-6

Ingredients:

- 1 Pound skinless, boneless, chicken breast, cubed
- 2 Tablespoons olive oil
- 2 lage onions, chopped
- 3 garlic cloves, minced
- 3 carrots, chopped
- 1 bay leaf
- 1 Teaspoon salt
- 1 Teaspoon poultry seasoning
- 8 Cups chicken broth
- 1/2 Cup dried split peas, washed and drained
- 1 Cup peas, thawed if frozen

Directions:

In a large soup pot, heat olive oil over medium heat. Add chicken and cook for 5 minutes, until lightly browned. Add onions, garlic, carrots, bay leaf, salt and seasoning and cook until vegetables soften, stirring occasionally. Add broth and split peas to pot and bring to a boil. Reduce heat, cover and simmer on low heat for 30-45 minutes. To the soup, add green peas and heat for 5 minutes, stirring to combine all ingredients.

Creamy Carrot Soup

You can adjust the amount of spice depending on the curry and there is a double dose of carrot flavor in this yummy soup.
Serves: 4-6

Ingredients:

- 2 Tablespoons olive oil
- 4 Cups carrots, chopped
- 1 onion, chopped
- 3 garlic cloves, minced
- 1 Tablespoon curry powder
- 3 Cups chicken broth
- 1 1/2 Cup carrot juice

Directions:

In a large soup pot, heat oil over medium heat. Add carrots and onion and continue to cook for about 6-8 minutes. Add garlic and curry powder and cook for another minute. Next, add broth and 1/2 tsp salt and simmer over low heat. Cover and let simmer for about 15 minutes. Add carrot juice and mix well. Puree the soup in a blender, working in batches. Return the soup to the pan and season with salt and pepper. Serve.

Note: for a richer texture, some cream can be mixed in.

Creamy Chickpea Soup

With a few accessible ingredients, you can have a fiber filled and flavorful soup. Fiber is recommended for those with diverticulosis.

Serves: 4

Ingredients:

- 2 1/2 Cups vegetable broth
- 2 Cups fresh baby spinach
- 2 Cups tomatoes, seeded and chopped
- 2 Cups hummus, homemade or store bought
- 1 Tablespoon lemon juice

Directions:

In a medium pot, bring vegetable broth to a boil. Add spinach and tomatoes and cook until spinach wilts, about 4 – 5 minutes. Lower heat and stir in the hummus and lemon juice and cook until heated through.

Creamy Squash Soup

Fiber is recommended for those with diverticulosis and this soup has lots of it with the combination of beans and vegetables.

Serves: 4-6

Ingredients:

- 1 acorn squash, cut lenthwise, seeds removed
- 1 sweet potato, cut lenghtwise
- 4 shallots, cut lengthwise
- 2 Tablespoons olive oil
- 4 garlic cloves, whole
- 4 Cups vegetable broth
- 14 Ounces cannellini beans, drained and rinsed
- 1/4 Cup sour cream

Directions:

Preheat oven to 375 degrees.

Brush cut sides of squash, sweet potato and shallots with oil. Place vegetables, cut side down, in a shallow roasting pan and add garlic cloves. Roast in oven until tender, about 30 – 40 minutes. Allow vegetables to cool, and scoop out flesh of squash, sweet potato. In a soup pot, place flesh of roasted vegetables, shallots and garlic. Add broth and bring to a boil. Reduce heat, and simmer, covered for 30 minutes, stirring occasionally. Pour half of the beans into the soup pot and allow soup to cool. Puree soup with a hand blender, until smooth. Add other half of beans and cream. Season to taste and simmer until warmed through, about 5 minutes. Serve.

Kidney Bean Soup

Beans are one of the highest sources of fiber, needed during diverticulosis. This soup is high fiber due to the beans and brown rice.

Serves: 4

Ingredients:

- 3 slices bacon
- 1 Teaspoon garlic cloves, minced
- 2 shallots, chopped
- 1 carrots, chopped
- 28 Ounces kidney beans, drained
- 1/2 Cup quick cooking brown rice
- 4 Cups beef broth
- 2 bay leaves
- 1/4 Teaspoon dried basil

Directions:

In a large soup pot, cook bacon over medium heat until crisp. Crumble and set aside. In the same pan with the bacon oil, cook garlic, shallots and carrots until tender, about 5 minutes. Place the beans in blender and puree until smooth. Stir into the vegetable mixture in the pan. Add the bacon, rice, broth, bay leaves and basil. Stir soup and bring pot to a boil. Reduce heat and simmer covered, until rice is tender, 20 minutes. Serve.

Lentil Soup

This lentil soup becomes creamy when the lentils and the potatoes soften. You won't realize how much fiber you are getting in this tasty soup.
Serves: 6

Ingredients:

- 2 Tablespoons olive oil
- 1 onion, chopped
- 2 carrots, chopped
- 2 celery stalks, chopped
- 3 medium potatoes, unpeeled, and cubed
- 2 bay leaf
- 2 Cups lentils, uncooked and rinsed
- 1/2 Teaspoon thyme
- 1/2 Teaspoon oregano
- 5 Cups vegetable broth
- 3 Cups water

Directions:

In a large soup pot, heat olive oil over medium- high heat.
Add onion, carrots, celery, and potatoes. Cook for 7-8 minutes or until tender. Add bay leaves, lentils, thyme and oregano. Cook for a few more minutes. Add vegetable broth and water, bring to a boil. Reduce heat to low and let simmer, covered for another 45 minutes, until lentils are soft and fall apart.

Mushroom and Ginger Soup

An Asian inspired soup with garlic and ginger may become a new favorite.
Serves: 4

Ingredients:

- 2 Teaspoons vegetable oil
- 3 garlic cloves, crushed
- 1 Tablespoon fresh ginger, grated
- 4 Ounces white mushrooms, sliced
- 4 Cups vegetable broth
- 1 Teaspoon low sodium soy sauce
- 4 Ounces bean sprouts
- 4 Ounces whole wheat thin pasta
- 4 Tablespoons fresh cilantro

Directions:

Bring a large pot of salted water to a boil. Add pasta and cook according to package instructions until al dente. Drain.

In a large soup pot, heat oil over medium-high heat. Add garlic, ginger and mushrooms. Stir until softened, about 3-4 minutes. Add vegetable stock and bring to boil. Add soy sauce and bean sprouts and continue to cook until tender. To serve, place cooked noodles in individual bowls and ladle soup on top. Garnish with fresh cilantro

Mushroom Barley Soup

Barley has a high fiber content, which is good for diverticulosis. This barley soup has a smoky flavor from the pancetta and the mushrooms.

Serves: 4

Ingredients:

- 3 Tablespoons olive oil
- 2 carrots, chopped
- 1 onion, chopped
- 5 Cups white mushrooms, sliced
- 3/4 Cups smoked ham or pancetta, diced
- 2 Teaspoons garlic cloves, minced
- 32 Ounces chicken broth
- 1/2 Cup quick cooking barley

Directions:

In a large soup pot, heat oil over medium-high heat. Add carrots and onion; cook, stirring occasionally until tender, about 5 minutes. Add mushrooms; cook, stirring frequently for 5 minutes. Add ham or pancetta, and garlic and cook about 5 more minutes. Add chicken broth, and barley. Bring to a boil; reduce heat and simmer covered, until barley is tender about 30 minutes. Serve.

Mushroom Barley Soup

Barley is high in fiber, recommended for diverticulosis. If the soup becomes thick the next day, you can thin it out with some broth or water.

Serves: 4

Ingredients:

- 2 Tablespoons olive oil
- 1 Cup carrots, chopped
- 1 Cup onion, chopped
- 1 Pound white mushrooms, sliced
- 1 1/2 Cup smoked ham, chopped
- 28 Ounces chicken broth
- 14 Ounces stewed tomatoes, seedless
- 1/2 Cup quick cooking barley

Directions:

In a large soup pot, heat olive oil over medium-high heat. Cook carrots and onion, stirring occasionally for about 5 minutes. Add mushrooms and cook, stirring frequently until mushrooms are tender, about 5 minutes. Add ham and cook stirring constantly for 1-2 minutes. Stir in chicken broth, tomatoes and barley. Bring pot to a boil, then reduce heat and simmer covered, until barley is tender, about 20 minutes.

Pea and Pesto Soup

Pesto, homemade or store bought gives this soup lots of flavor and the split peas provide lots of fiber. A high fiber diet is recommended during diverticulosis.
Serves: 2

Ingredients:

- 1 Cup yellow split peas, uncooked, rinsed
- 2 Cups chicken broth
- 2 1/2 Cups water
- 2 Tablespoons pesto, homemade or store bought
- 1 small zucchini, seeded and sliced
- 1/2 Cup green onions, chopped

Directions:

In a large soup pot, combine split peas, broth and water and bring to a boil. Reduce heat, cover, and simmer for 20 minutes.

Stir in pesto, zucchini, and green onions; simmer for 15 to 20 more minutes. Garnish with Parmesan cheese, if desired.

Slow Cooker Lentil, Sausage and Kale Soup

A hearty and tasty soup that can easily be made in a slow cooker.
Serves: 4
Equipment: slow cooker
Cook Time: 6h 0m

Ingredients:

- 2 Tablespoons olive oil
- 1 Pound Italian seasoned turkey sausage, casings removed
- 1 onion, chopped
- 2 carrots, chopped
- 2 celery stalks, chopped
- 1 Teaspoon Italian seasoning
- 1/2 Teaspoon black pepper
- 2 garlic cloves, chopped
- 15 Ounces diced tomatoes
- 1 1/2 Cup green or brown lentils
- 4 Cups vegetable or chicken broth
- 3 Cups kale, chopped roughly

Directions:

In a slow cooker, heat the olive oil and brown/sear the Italian turkey sausage, crumbling with a wooden spoon. Add onions, carrots, celery, and Italian seasoning and pepper, and cook until vegetables soften about 5-7 minutes. Add garlic and cook another minute.
Add tomatoes, lentils, and broth and stir to combine all ingredients.
Cook covered on low for 6-8 hours, until lentils get tender, not mushy.
Add kale and stir and cook until kale wilts. Adjust seasoning.
Serve with grated Parmesan on top if desired and crusty whole-wheat bread.
Note- If the slow cooker does not have a sear/browning function, the sausage and vegetables and seasonings can be cooked in a separate skillet and then added to the slow cooker.

Smooth Broccoli Soup

Broccoli is a good source of fiber and paired with unpeeled potatoes, this soup has lots of fiber.
Serves: 4

Ingredients:

- 2 Tablespoons olive oil
- 1 leek, choppped
- 1 celery stalk, chopped
- 2 garlic cloves, minced
- 3 small potatoes, unpeeled, chopped
- 1/2 Teaspoon salt
- 1 bay leaf
- 3 Cups vegetable broth
- 1 1/2 Cup broccoli florets

Directions:

In a large soup pan, heat oil over medium-high heat. Cook leek, celery, garlic, potatoes, salt and bay leaf until lightly browned. Add stock and bring to a boil. Reduce heat, cover and simmer 30 minutes. Add broccoli florets to pot and bring back to a boil. Reduce heat, cover, and simmer another 15 minutes or until all vegetables are tender. Remove from heat and let cool. Remove bay leaf. Puree soup with a hand blender, until smooth. Serve.

Split Pea Soup

Split peas are one of the highest sources of fiber, which is recommended during diverticulosis. This soup is blended so it has a creamy texture.
Serves: 4

Ingredients:

- 1 Tablespoon olive oil
- 1 onion, chopped
- 1 celery stalk, chopped
- 1 carrot, chopped
- 1 red bell pepper, seeded, chopped
- 1 Cup yellow split peas, uncooked, rinsed
- 3 1/2 Cups chicken broth
- 3 Cups water
- 1/4 Cup plain yogurt

Directions:

In a large soup pot, heat olive oil over medium-high heat.
Add onion, celery, carrot, and red peppers. Cook for 7 -8 minutes or until tender. Add split peas, chicken broth and water, bring to a boil. Reduce heat to low and let simmer, covered for 45 minutes or until peas have fallen apart. Puree soup a hand blender until smooth. Garnish with a dollop of yogurt if desired. Serve.

SALAD RECIPES

Asian Chicken Salad

This is a refreshing an easy salad to make and chicken breast can be substituted with sliced beef or fish.
Serves: 1

Ingredients:

- 1 Cup romaine lettuce, chopped
- 1 carrot, shredded
- 1 celery, sliced thinly
- 1/4 Cup red bell pepper, seeded, sliced thinly
- 1/2 Cup chicken breast, cut into strips
- 1/4 Cup mangoes
- 2 Tablespoons lime and ginger dressing, store bought

Directions:

In a medium bowl, toss together all ingredients until combined. Serve alone or with whole wheat bread slices.

Bean and Couscous Salad

A great way to get lots of fiber which is recommended with diverticulosis.

Serves: 4

Ingredients:

- 1 Cup couscous
- 1 1/2 Cup boiling water
- 1 Cup yellow bell peppers, seeded and chopped
- 2 Cups cooked black beans
- 1 small onion, chopped
- 2 Cups tomatoes, seeded and chopped
- 2 garlic cloves, minced
- 1/2 Cup rice vinegar
- 1/4 Cup olive oil
- 1/2 Teaspoon salt
- 1/4 Teaspoon pepper

Directions:

In a large bowl, place the couscous with boiling water. Cover and wait until couscous has absorbed all the water. Add the remaining ingredients. Mix well and season with salt and pepper. Serve.

Brown Rice Greek Salad

This Greek-inspired salad with rice can be served warm or cold and with or without whole wheat pita bread.

Serves: 2

Ingredients:

- 1/2 Cup Brown rice, cooked
- 1/2 Cup white beans, canned, drained, rinsed
- 1/2 Cup fresh spinach
- 1/2 Cup tomatoes, no seeds
- 1/2 Cup English Cucumber, no seeds
- 1/4 Cup avocado, diced
- 1 Tablespoon red onion, chopped
- 2 Tablespoons Feta cheese, crumbled
- 2 Tablespoons extra virgin olive oil
- 1 Teaspoon red wine vinegar
- to taste salt and pepper

Directions:

In a medium bowl, combine brown rice, beans, spinach, tomatoes, cucumber, avocado, onion, and cheese until combined. Drizzle oil and vinegar on top and season to taste with salt and pepper. Toss together. Can be served alone or with whole wheat pita bread.

Chicken Pasta Salad

This salad is a rounded meal with the fiber, protein, and vegetables. A high fiber diet is recommended for those with diverticulosis.

Serves: 4

Ingredients:

- 1/2 Pound whole wheat pasta
- 1 Cup cooked chicken breast, cubed
- 10 Ounces frozed broccoli, thawed and drained
- 1/2 Cup peas, thawed from frozen
- 1/2 Cup Ranch dressing
- 1 Teaspoon Italian seasoning
- 1 Tablespoon Parmesan cheese, grated

Directions:

Bring a large pot of salted water to a boil. Add pasta and cook according to package instructions until al dente. Drain.

Combine cooked pasta with chicken, broccoli and peas. Set aside. In a separate bowl, blend together dressing, herbs and cheese. Pour dressing mixture into pasta and vegetable mixture. Toss well to coat, and serve.

Cilantro Bean Salad

A colorful and tasty way to get lots of fiber in your diet. The dressing is filled with lots of fresh flavor.
Serves: 2-4

Ingredients:

- 14 Ounces can kidney beans, drained and rinsed
- 14 Ounces can garbanzo beans, drained and rinsed
- 1 medium red onion, diced
- 1 small red bell pepper, seeded and chopped
- 1 Cup fresh cilantro
- 1/2 Cup balsamic vinegar
- 1 Tablespoon Dijon mustard
- 1 1/2 Teaspoon cumin
- 3 garlic cloves
- 1/2 Teaspoon salt
- 1 1/2 Cup olive oil
- 1/2 lemon, juiced

Directions:

In a medium bowl, combine beans, onion and bell pepper and set aside.
In a food processor, blend the rest of the ingredients until smooth. Pour half of the dressing over bean mixture and combine. Refrigerate at least one hour.
Pour remaining dressing over salad and mix gently just before serving. Serve at room temperature.

Fruit Salad with Avocado

This is a sweet and refreshing way to get fiber and vitamins at lunch or as a side salad at dinner.
Serves: 4

Ingredients:

- 2 large avocados, pitted and diced
- 1 peach, unpeeled, pitted and diced
- 1 apple, unpeeled, cored and diced
- 1 Cup cantaloupe, chopped
- 1 shallot, chopped finely
- 1 English cucumber, seedless, chopped
- 1/4 Cup fresh lime juice
- 1/4 Cup fresh mint, chopped
- 8 large lettuce leaves

Directions:

In a medium bowl, combine all ingredients except the lettuce leaves. Sprinkle with lime juice and mint and toss together to combine. Let salad sit at least 10-20 minutes. Serve over 2 leaves of lettuce per serving.

Garbanzo and Tomato Salad

A Mediterranean inspired salad with a lot of fiber and flavor. Cannellini beans can be substituted for the garbanzo beans.

Serves: 4

Ingredients:

- 4 Ounces medium tomatoes, seeded and chopped
- 28 Ounces can garbanzo beans, drained and rinsed
- 1/4 Cup red onion, chopped finely
- 1 Cup Italian parsley, chopped finely
- 2 Tablespoons lemon juice
- 1/4 Cup olive oil
- 1/2 Teaspoon salt
- 1/4 Teaspoon pepper

Directions:

In a large bowl, combine tomatoes, garbanzo beans, onions and fresh parsley. Set aside. In a separate small bowl whisk together lemon juice, olive oil and salt. Pour dressing over vegetables. Mix and serve.

Greek White Bean and Feta Salad

The freshly made dressing turns this salad into a tasty and fresh treat any time of the year.
Serves: 6

Ingredients:

- 2 Tablespoons plain yogurt
- 3 Tablespoons olive oil
- 2 Tablespoons fresh lemon juice
- 3/4 Teaspoons oregano
- 1 Tablespoon fresh mint, chopped
- 28 Ounces white cannellini beans, drained and rinsed
- 1/2 Cup red onion, chopped finely
- 3 medium tomatoes, seeded and chopped
- 1/4 Cup Greek olives, pitted
- 1/2 Cup feta cheese,crumbled
- 2 Cups fresh spinach leaves, torn

Directions:

In large bowl, combine yogurt, olive oil, lemon juice, oregano, and mint ; whisk well. Add beans, onion, tomato, olives and feta cheese; toss lightly. Refrigerate for at least one hour. Serve on a bed of spinach.

Green Bean Potato Salad

The green beans and keeping the potatoes unpeeled add the needed fiber in this non-traditional potato salad.

Serves: 4-6

Ingredients:

- 1 1/2 Pound fresh green beans
- 6 small red potatoes, unpeeled, cubed
- 1 small onion, thinly sliced
- 1/3 Cup olive oil
- 1/4 Cup red wine vinegar
- 1/4 Cup rice vinegar
- 1 Tablespoon garlic powder
- 1 Teaspoon sugar

Directions:

In a large pot of boiling water, cook green beans and potatoes about 7 minutes or until crisp-tender. Drain and place only the beans in cold water to stop cooking process. Drain and set aside. In a large salad bowl, combine green beans, potatoes and onions.

For dressing, in a small bowl, whisk together olive oil, vinegars, garlic powder and sugar. Pour dressing over vegetables and toss to coat well. Refrigerate one hour prior to serving.

Green Bean Tuna Salad

You will want to make this salad especially when green beans are in season, but it is yummy any time of the year. The fresh tarragon gives it a special touch.
Serves: 4

Ingredients:

- 3 Pounds green beans
- 1/2 Cup mayonnaise
- 1/3 Cup tarragon vinegar
- 1 Teaspoon Dijon mustard
- small shallots, sliced thinly
- 12 Ounces tuna fish, drained
- small sprigs tarragon, chopped finely

Directions:

In a large pot of boiling water, add green beans. Reduce heat to low, cover and simmer 5-10 minutes until beans are tender. Drain and place beans in cold water to stop cooking process. Drain and set aside. In a large bowl, combine mayonnaise, vinegar and mustard. Add green beans, shallots and tuna fish; toss to coat with dressing. Cover and refrigerate one hour prior to serving.
Garnish with fresh tarragon and serve.

Grilled Shrimp and Bean Salad

This is a quick and easy dish that has lots of texture, flavor and fiber. The shrimp can be substituted with fish or tofu for a light salad.
Serves: 6

Ingredients:

- 1 1/2 Pound shrimp, peeled, cleaned, and deveined,
- 1/2 Cup olive oil
- 2 garlic cloves, minced
- 1/2 Teaspoon salt
- 2 small shallots, sliced thinly
- 1 Tablespoon fresh Italian parsley, chopped
- 1 1/2 Tablespoon fresh basil, chopped
- 1 Tablespoon red wine vinegar
- 28 Ounces white cannellini beans, drained and rinsed

Directions:

In a shallow glass dish, combine 1/4 cup of the olive oil with the garlic and 1/4 teaspoon of the salt. Add the shrimp and mix well. Set aside. In a medium bowl, combine the shallots with the remaining 1/4 cup oil and 1/4 teaspoon salt, parsley, basil, and vinegar. Gently stir in the beans.
Grill the shrimp over medium-high heat, turning once, until just done, about 3-5 minutes. Serve the shrimp with the bean salad.

Grilled Steak and Mixed Greens Salad

The addition of beans and vegetables make this a high fiber salad and filling as well.
Serves: 4

Ingredients:

- 1 Pound sirloin steak, boneless, 1/2 inch thick
- 1 Cup Italian salad dressing, homemade or store bought
- 8 Ounces mixed salad greens
- 2 medium tomatoes, seeded and chopped
- 1 Cup white beans, cooked or canned, rinsed and drained
- 1 medium carrot, shredded
- 1 celery, sliced thinly
- 1 medium summer squash or zucchini, shredded

Directions:

Marinade steak with1/2 cup of the dressing in a bowl and cover. Let marinate in refrigerator for 30 minutes. Grill steak over high heat for 5-10 minutes to desired doneness. Set steak aside and let rest 10 minutes. Meanwhile, toss greens with tomatoes, beans, carrot, celery, squash and remaining 1/2 cup of dressing. Cut steak across the grain into thin slices. Place vegetables on serving platter. Top with steak slices, serve.

Lentil Tomato Salad

A healthy lentil salad packed with flavor and protein! Perfect for quick lunches or snacks.
Serves: 4 People
Prep time: 5m

Ingredients:

- 15 Ounces Can Lentils
- 1.5 Cups Cherry Tomatoes
- 1/4 Cup White Wine Vinegar
- 1/8 Cup Chives (optional)

Directions:

Drain and rinse the lentils. Cut cherry tomatoes in half. Slice optional chives.
Add all ingredients to a bowl and toss to fully combine. Add salt and adjust vinegar to your taste.
Serve immediately or refrigerate in a covered container to let flavors develop more. Optional additions: olive oil, basil, parsley

Light Shrimp and Barley Salad

An very versatile and easy to make recipe with lots of delicate seafood flavor. The barley provides lots of fiber, which is recommended for those with diverticulosis.

Serves: 4

Ingredients:

- 1 Cup barley
- 2 Cups chicken broth
- 1/2 Cup shrimp, peeled, deveined, and cooked
- 1 medium green pepper, seeded and chopped
- 1 Teaspoon Dijon mustard
- 1/2 Cup mayonnaise
- 1/2 Cup fresh basil, chopped

Directions:

In a medium saucepan, bring barley and chicken broth to a boil. Reduce heat and simmer for 30 - 40 minutes, or until the barley is tender. Drain well and fluff with a fork.

In a large serving bowl, combine the barley, shrimp, green pepper, mustard, mayonnaise and basil, and chill at least 30 minutes. Garnish with fresh basil. Serve.

Mango Black Bean Salad

Black beans are an excellent source of fiber, needed in the diverticulosis diet. The fresh mango and herbs provide flavor and freshness.

Serves: 6

Ingredients:

- 28 Ounces black beans, drained and rinsed
- 4 medium mangoes, peeled and diced
- 1 Cup fresh Italian parsley, chopped
- 2 small scallions, chopped finely
- 2 medium red peppers, seeded and diced
- 2 Tablespoons olive oil
- 1/2 Cup balsamic vinegar
- 1/4 Teaspoon salt

Directions:

In a large salad bowl, combine beans with mangoes, parsley, scallions, and red bell peppers. In a separate small bowl, whisk together the oil, vinegar and salt. Pour over vegetables and mix well. Serve.

Mediterranean Salmon and Potato Salad

A delicious salad with lots of fiber from the beans and the unpeeled potatoes. The salmon can substituted with any type of fish of your choice.
Serves: 4

Ingredients:

- 1 Pound red potatoes, unpeeled, cut into wedges
- 1/2 Cup olive oil
- 2 Tablespoons balsamic vinegar
- 1 Tablespoon rosemary, minced
- 2 Cups white cannellini beans, drained and rinsed
- 4 salmon fillets, 4 oz each
- 2 Tablespoons lemon juice
- 1/4 Teaspoon salt
- 8 large lettuce leaves, torn
- 2 Cups English cucumber, seedless, sliced

Directions:

In a medium saucepan, bring water to a boil and cook potatoes until tender, about 10 minutes. Drain and pour potatoes back into pan.

To make dressing, in a small bowl, whisk together 1/2 cup of olive oil, vinegar and rosemary. Combine potatoes and white beans with dressing. Set aside.

In a separate medium pan, heat the remaining 2 tbs of olive oil over medium-high heat. Add salmon fillets and sprinkle with lemon juice and salt. Cook about 5-7 minutes on each side or until fish flakes easily. To serve, place lettuce and cucumber slices on a serving platter top with potato salad and fish fillets.

Mixed Bean Salad

A classic bean salad with plenty of fiber which is good for diverticulosis and a twist of flavor with the artichokes.
Serves: 6

Ingredients:

- 15 Ounces green beans, drained and rinsed
- 15 Ounces wax beans, drained and rinsed
- 15 Ounces kidney beans, drained and rinsed
- 15 Ounces garbanzo beans, drained and rinsed
- 1/4 Cup red onion, chopped
- 8 Ounces artichokes, marinated, chopped
- 1/4 Cup fresh orange juice
- 1/2 Cup cider vinegar
- 1/2 Cup olive oil

Directions:

In a large serving bowl, combine all of the beans, onion, and artichokes. In a separate small bowl, mix together the juice and vinegar and olive oil. Pour dressing over bean mixture. Stir to coat. Let marinate in refrigerator for 30 minutes prior to serving.

Quick Spinach and Black Bean Salad

You do not need much time to throw this salad together. Can also be topped with grilled chicken for added protein.
Serves: 4

Ingredients:

- 2 Cups black beans,cooked, drained, and rinsed
- 1/4 Cup green onions, chopped finely
- 10 Ounces fresh spinach
- red pepper, seeded, and chopped
- yellow pepper, seeded and chopped
- 1/2 Cup feta, crumbled
- 1 Cup Italian dressing

Directions:

In a medium bowl, combine beans, onions, spinach, peppers and cheese. Pour dressing on top and mix together until combined

Red Beans and Pickle Salad

A simple, tasty salad or relish with lots of fiber and flavor.
Serves: 4

Ingredients:

- 28 Ounces red beans, drained and rinsed
- 1/4 Cup water chestnuts, drained and chopped
- red onion, chopped
- 1/4 Cup pickles, sliced
- 1/2 Cup olive oil
- 1/4 Cup balsamic vinegar
- 1/4 Teaspoon salt

Directions:

In a medium bowl, combine red beans, water chestnuts, onion, and pickles. Set aside. In a small bowl, whisk together the olive oil, vinegar and salt. Pour over bean mix and serve.

Shrimp, Pasta and Spinach Salad

This satisfying salad can be made with chicken as well. The whole wheat pasta provides some of the fiber needed in the diverticulosis phase.

Serves: 2

Ingredients:

- 1/2 Pound whole wheat pasta
- 3/4 Pounds medium shrimp, cooked
- 2 Cups fresh spinach
- Roma tomatoes, seeded and chopped
- 1/2 Cup Ranch salad dressing
- 4 Tablespoons fresh basil, chopped
- 1/4 Cup Parmesan cheese, grated

Directions:

Bring a large pot of salted water to a boil. Cook pasta according to package instructions until al dente. Drain. While pasta is cooking, in a large bowl, combine shrimp, spinach, tomatoes, salad dressing and cooked pasta. Refrigerate for 20 minutes. Toss together with basil and cheese. Serve.

Spinach and Apple Salad

Serves: 2

Ingredients:

- 1/2 Pound fresh spinach
- 1/2 Cup cabbage, thinly sliced
- pear, unpeeled, thinly sliced
- 1/4 Cup green onions, chopped finely
- 1 Tablespoon fresh basil, chopped
- 2 Teaspoons balsamic vinegar
- 1/3 Cup fresh orange juice
- 1/4 Cup olive oil

Directions:

In a large salad bowl, combine the spinach, cabbage, and pear. To make dressing, in a small bowl, whisk together the green onions, basil, balsamic vinegar, orange juice and olive oil. Pour dressing over salad. Serve.

Tuna and Bean Salad

This salad is so versatile, it can be made with chicken instead of tuna and any variety of leafy green besides arugula. The beans can be of your choice as well since beans provide lots of fiber.
Serves: 4

Ingredients:

- 28 Ounces cannellini beans
- 4 Cups arugula
- 12 Ounces tuna fish, drained
- 4 Tablespoons olive oil
- 2 Tablespoons lemon juice
- 1/4 Teaspoon salt
- 1 Tablespoon Italian parsley, chopped
- 1/2 Cup green onions, chopped finely

Directions:

Place beans into serving dish. Pour the tuna evenly over the beans. Place the arugula on top of the tuna. In a separate, small bowl, prepare the dressing by whisking together the oil, lemon juice, salt and parsley until well combined. Pour dressing over the tuna and beans. Sprinkle onions over the bean salad and mix well. Serve.

Veggie and Rice Salad

This colorful and flavorful salad will be a favorite. The unpeeled potatoes and brown rice provide lots of fiber recommended during diverticulosis.
Serves: 6

Ingredients:

- 1 1/2 Teaspoon olive oil
- green bell peppers, seeded and chopped
- 1 Cup green beans, chopped
- onion, chopped
- carrots, chopped
- 1 Cup mushrooms, sliced
- potatoes, unpeeled, cooked, cubed
- 1/2 Teaspoon cumin
- 1/2 Teaspoon oregano
- 1 1/2 Tablespoon soy sauce, low sodium
- 3 Cups instant brown rice, cooked and cooled
- 1/4 Cup Italian parsley, chopped
- 2 Tablespoons lemon juice

Directions:

In a large non-stick pan, heat olive oil over medium-high heat.
Cook peppers, green beans, onions, and carrots for about 7 minutes. Add mushrooms and potatoes and continue cooking
2 - 3 minutes. Add cumin, oregano and soy sauce. Transfer mixture to a large salad bowl and allow to cool to room temperature. Add rice, chopped parsley and lemon juice. Mix together until combined. Serve.

SNACK RECIPES

Baked Sweet Potato Fries

These yummy fries are a much healthier alternative to traditional fries since they still have the peel on that provides fiber.
Serves: 4

Ingredients:

- 4 small sweet potatoes, unpeeled
- 1 Tablespoon butter, melted
- 1/4 Teaspoon salt
- dash of nutmeg

Directions:

Preheat oven to 450F degrees.
Spray a large baking pan with non-stick cooking spray. Scrub potatoes and cut lengthwise into quarters, then cut each quarter into 2 wedges. Arrange potatoes in a single layer in pan. In a small bowl, combine butter, salt, and nutmeg. Brush mixture onto potatoes and coat evenly. Bake in oven 20 minutes or until brown and tender.

Citrus Carrots

This can be served as a side dish or enjoyed as a snack. The carrots and orange provide some fiber.
Serves: 3

Ingredients:

- 1 Pound baby carrots
- 2 Tablespoons balsamic vinegar
- 1/2 Cup orange juice
- 1 orange, peeled and chopped
- 1 Tablespoon green onions, chopped finely
- 1 Tablespoon fresh dill, chopped

Directions:

Steam carrots in a steamer until tender or plunge carrots into boiling water and cook for about 10 - 12 minutes until tender.

Drain. Rinse with cold water and drain again.

In a medium bowl, combine carrots, vinegar and orange juice. Stir to combine. Add orange segments, onions and dill. Lightly toss and serve.

Greek Lettuce Wraps

A quick and easy snack to pull together and still get some fiber.
Serves: 2

Ingredients:

- 1/4 Cup mayonnaise
- 2 Teaspoons lemon juice
- 1/2 Cup white beans, drained and rinsed
- 1/3 Cup feta cheese,crumbled
- 2 Tablespoons pimentos, chopped
- 8 large lettuce leaves
- 1/2 Pound cooked chicken breast, cubed

Directions:

In a medium bowl, combine mayonnaise and lemon juice. Stir in beans, mashing slightly with fork. Add cheese and pimentos, and mix lightly. Spread lettuce leaves evenly with bean mixture.
Top with chicken; roll up. Serve.

Honey Baked Apples

This snack can also be made with any type of apple or even with pears. Foods have more fiber when the skin is not peeled off. Fiber is important in the diverticulosis diet.
Serves: 4

Ingredients:

- 4 apples, unpeeled
- 1/4 Cup brown sugar
- 1/2 Teaspoon ground cloves
- 1/2 Teaspoon cinnamon
- 1/2 Cup honey
- 1/2 Cup water

Directions:

Preheat oven to 400 degrees.

Core and slice apples into 1/2" rings. Place them in a shallow baking dish for later use. In a small saucepan, combine and heat brown sugar, cloves, cinnamon, honey and water. Pour over apples and bake 15 minutes or until tender, turning to baste once or twice. Serve.

Kidney Bean Salsa

This twist to traditional salsa adds fiber from the beans and yellow pepper. Tastes better if allowed to sit for about 30 minutes.

Serves: 4

Ingredients:

- 14 Ounces red kidney beans, drained and rinsed
- 2 tomatoes, seeded and chopped
- 1 yellow bell pepper, seeded and chopped
- 1 avocado, chopped
- 1 Tablespoon cilantro, chopped
- 2 Tablespoons lime juice
- 1/4 Teaspoon salt

Directions:

In large bowl, mix all ingredients until combined well.

Serve with warm tortillas or whole wheat chips.

Oatmeal Chocolate Chip Cookies

Sometimes you just crave something sweet but don't want all the extra fat, sugar and preservatives. These are easy to make and you get 1 gram of fiber per cookie.
Serves: 24 cookies

Ingredients:

- 1/3 Cup brown sugar
- 1/2 Cup butter, softened
- 1/2 Teaspoon vanilla extract
- 1 egg
- 1 Cup whole grain, rolled oats
- 3/4 Cups whole wheat flour
- 1/2 Teaspoon baking soda
- 1/2 Cup dark chocolate chips

Directions:

Heat oven to 350 degrees. In a large bowl, cream brown sugar and butter until well combined. Stir in vanilla and egg and mix until light and fluffy. Stir in rolled oats, whole wheat flour, baking soda and fold in chocolate chips. Onto a cookie sheet covered with a Silpat mat or foil, drop the dough by rounded tablespoons (you can also use an ice cream scooper) about 2 inches apart.
Bake 10-12 minutes or until golden brown. Cool slightly; remove from cookie sheet to a wire rack.

White Bean Puree

An easy to make appetizer or snack that can be made all in a food processor within minutes. This is another high fiber alternative to traditional dips.

Serves: 4

Ingredients:

- 14 Ounces cannellini beans, drained and rinsed
- 2 garlic cloves
- 1/4 Cup fresh Italian parsley
- 1/2 lemon, juiced
- 1/4 Teaspoon oregano
- 1/2 Teaspoon salt
- 1/3 Cup olive oil

Directions:

Blend all ingredients in a food processor until almost smooth. Serve with crusty bread, whole wheat crackers, or fresh vegetables

HOLIDAY RECIPES

Baked Artichoke Dip

An easy to make warm dip that can be prepared ahead of time. The beans and artichokes provide fiber in this yummy dip.

Serves: 4

Ingredients:

- 14 Ounces artichokes, drained and chopped
- 14 Ounces cannellini beans, drained and rinsed
- 1/2 Cup mayonnaise
- 1/2 Cup plain Greek yogurt
- 1 Cup Parmesan cheese, grated
- 10 Ounces frozen spinach, thawed and chopped
- 1/2 Cup red bell pepper, seeded and chopped
- 1/4 Cup Mozzarella cheese, shredded

Directions:

Heat oven to 350°F. Mix artichokes, beans, mayonnaise, Greek yogurt, and Parmesan cheese. Stir in spinach and bell pepper.

Spoon mixture into 1-quart casserole. Sprinkle with Mozzarella cheese.

Cover and bake about 20 minutes or until cheese is melted. Serve warm with vegetables or whole wheat baguette slices.

Bean and Tomato Salad

A fresh and easy to make salad for the holidays or any time of the year. The beans provide fiber and creaminess and the tomatoes add a fresh touch. Beans are one of the best sources of fiber, needed for diverticulosis.

Serves: 3-4

Ingredients:

- 28 Ounces white beans, drained and rinsed
- 2 Cups green beans, cut into 1 inch pieces
- 2 Cups tomatoes, seeded and chopped
- 1/2 Cup Italian dressing
- 2 Tablespoons fresh basil, chopped
- 2 Tablespoons Parmesan cheese, grated

Directions:

In a medium serving bowl, combine first four ingredients together. Garnish with basil and cheese. Can be served with whole wheat pita bread triangles.

Broccoli and Potato Casserole

This recipe has a lot fiber but also has a rich texture and delicious flavor. It will become a holiday favorite.
Serves: 4-6

Ingredients:

- 6 Pieces red potatoes, unpeeled and cubed
- 2 Cups broccoli, chopped
- 4 Tablespoons butter
- 4 garlic cloves, minced
- 1/2 Cup heavy cream
- 1/2 Cup cheddar cheese
- 1/2 Tablespoon salt
- 1/4 Teaspoon nutmeg

Directions:

Place potatoes in a pot and cover with water. Add salt to water and boil potatoes until almost tender, about 6 to 8 minutes. Add broccoli and cook until tender, an additional 5-7 minutes.

Drain potatoes and broccoli. Melt butter in the hot pot, then add the garlic and cook 2 to 3 minutes. Stir in cream; add potatoes, broccoli and cheese and season with salt, pepper and nutmeg. Mash until desired consistency.

Delicious Sweet Potatoes

Sweet potatoes are usually a holiday favorite and this recipe will not disappoint. The freshness of the orange juice and lemon zest give a fresh twist. Sweet potatoes are naturally high in fiber, so it is a recommended food for diverticulosis.

Serves: 6-8

Ingredients:

- 4 Pounds sweet potatoes, peeled and cut into large bite size pieces
- 2 Cups orange juice
- 1/2 Cup honey
- 1 Teaspoon cinnamon
- 1 Teaspoon nutmeg
- 2 Tablespoons vanilla extract
- 2 Teaspoons lemon zest
- 2 Tablespoons flour
- 1/2 Cupbrown sugar

Directions:

Preheat oven to 350 degrees. Boil sweet potatoes until slightly underdone. Drain, cool and set aside. In a large bowl, whisk together orange juice, cinnamon, nutmeg, vanilla and zest. In another bowl, combine flour and both sugar together. Put cooled sweet potatoes in a deep baking dish, add dry ingredient mixture and stir to coat. Pour liquid over sweet potatoes and bake for 20 to 25 minutes.

Easy Creamy Pumpkin Soup

Pumpkin has a good amount of fiber content, making it a good choice for a holiday soup…healthy and festive.

Serves: 4

Ingredients:

- 1 Tablespoon olive oil
- 1/4 Cup onion, chopped
- 1 Tablespoon curry powder
- 15 Ounces pumpkin puree
- 2 Cups vegetable broth
- 2 Tablespoons maple syrup
- 1/2 Tablespoon salt
- 14 Ounces unsweetened coconut milk
- 4 Teaspoons sour cream, optional

Directions:

In a large pot, heat oil over medium heat. Add the onion. Cover and cook until softened, 5 minutes. Stir in curry powder and the pumpkin puree, then whisk in the broth until smooth. Add the maple syrup and season with salt. Simmer for 10 minutes, stirring occasionally.

Using a hand-held blender, puree the soup in the pot. Otherwise, transfer the soup to a blender or food processor and puree until smooth. Stir back into the pot. Reduce heat to low. Whisk in the coconut milk, Heat until hot, but, do not boil.

Soup can be topped with a teaspoon dollop of sour cream if desired.

Holiday Stuffing

This holiday stuffing is festive yet has a good amount of fiber provided by the wheat bread and unpeeled apples. Fiber is an important part of preventing diverticulosis.
Serves: 4

Ingredients:

- 1 loaf whole wheat bread, cubed
- 3/4 stick unsalted butter
- 3 large tart apples, unpeeled, chopped
- 1 onion, chopped
- 3 celery stalks, chopped
- 2 Cups chicken broth
- 1/2 Cup dried apricots
- 1/2 Cup prunes, chopped
- 1/2 Cup fresh Italian parsley
- 1/2 Tablespoon salt

Directions:

Preheat oven to 400 degrees. Lay cubed bread on a baking sheet in a single layer and bake, until toasted, about 10 minutes. Allow to cool. While bread is toasting, prepare fruit mixture. Heat butter in a large pan over medium- high heat. Add apples, onion, and celery and cook until softened, about 8-10 minutes. Put mixture in a large bowl and combine with toasted bread, broth, apricots, prunes, parsley and salt. Transfer mixture to a 3-quart baking dish and cover with foil. Bake 20 minutes, remove foil and bake an additional 15 minutes

Spinach and Mushroom Toss

This is a good side dish to have during the holidays or any time of the year.
Serves: 4

Ingredients:

- 2 Teaspoons olive oil
- 1/4 Cup shallots, minced
- 3 garlic cloves, minced
- 3 bacon strips, chopped
- 4 Cups white mushrooms, sliced
- 3 Tablespoons balsamic vinegar
- 1 1/2 Tablespoon low sodium soy sauce
- 20 Ounces fresh baby spinach

Directions:

In a large pan, heat olive oil over medium heat. Add shallots and garlic and cook for 1 minute. Add bacon and cook an additional 2-3 minutes, or until browned. Add mushrooms and cook 3 to 5 minutes, until mushrooms are tender. Add balsamic vinegar and soy sauce and bring to a simmer. Add spinach and simmer 1 to 2 minutes, until spinach wilts, turning frequently.

RECIPES INDEX

Lightning Source UK Ltd.
Milton Keynes UK
UKHW050808241022
410994UK00009B/569